Omar's

Patricia Almada
Illustrated by Monique Passicot

Rigby

"It's time to go to the park for the soccer game," said Dad.

"Get ready, everyone!"
said Mom.

Carlos put on his soccer shirt.
Dora put on her soccer shoes.

4

Omar put on his soccer cap.

"I have the food and
the water," said Mom.

"I have the blanket and the umbrella," said Dad.

"Come on!" said Dora.

"I see the team!"
shouted Carlos.

Dora and Carlos ran to play
with the team.

8

Mom and Dad sat
on the blanket.
Omar looked very sad.

Omar said, "I want to play."

"You are too little," said Mom.

"You can play when you are eight years old," said Dad.

"Good kick, Dora!" yelled Dad.

Omar kicked, too.

"Oh, here comes the ball!" shouted Mom.

"Watch out!" said Dad.

Omar saw the ball.
He kicked it very hard!

Omar made a goal.
"Great kick, Omar!"
everyone said.